The 5 Powerful Habits of Successful People

Foreword:

Success is something that we all strive for, but few of us achieve it. What sets successful people apart? The answer lies in their habits and mindset. In this book, we will explore five powerful habits that successful people have mastered to achieve their goals.

Chapter 1 delves into the importance of planning. Successful people understand the value of creating a roadmap and leaving nothing to chance. Planning allows them to stay focused on their goals and take the necessary steps to achieve them.

Chapter 2 explores the habit of being observant and inspired. Successful people have a knack for spotting opportunities that others might miss. They also constantly seek inspiration to fuel their creativity and passion.

Chapter 3 emphasizes the need to prioritize mental and physical health. Successful people understand that taking care of their well-being is essential for success. They prioritize self-care, which allows them to stay focused, energized, and productive.

Chapter 4 focuses on the habit of staying true to one's path. Successful people are determined and unwavering in their pursuit of their goals. They understand that success is a journey and stay committed to their path, even when faced with challenges.

Chapter 5 highlights the importance of living in the moment. Successful people approach each day with enthusiasm, seeing it as an opportunity to learn and grow. They embrace life fully and make the most of every moment.

In this book, you will learn how to cultivate these five powerful habits in your own life. These habits will help you unlock your potential and achieve success in all areas of your life. So, get ready to be inspired and start your journey to success today!

My story is one of struggle and redemption, of hitting rock bottom and rising up to become a true inspiration for those who have faced similar challenges. After dedicating myself to a career that promised so much but left me high and dry, I finally had enough. I knew that it was time to do some real heavy self-evaluation and improvement, to step up into my better self and make the life I always knew was out there.

Despite facing numerous setbacks, including failing at over six businesses, I refused to give up. Instead, I focused on implementing strong work habits and mental reconditioning to emerge as a leader in my field. And it was my unwavering determination that led me to develop a breakthrough product that made real headway.

But my journey was not an easy one. Coming from a middle-class background where I often felt misunderstood and like an outcast, I had to persevere and overcome countless obstacles to achieve success. And now, through my book "The 5 Powerful Habits of Successful People," I share my story and the strategies I used to overcome my challenges.

My story is a testament to the power of determination and resilience, and it serves as a beacon of hope for anyone struggling to get their life together. I know firsthand the pain and suffering that can come with trying to achieve success, but I also know that it's possible to rise above it all and achieve greatness. My book is a guide for anyone looking to take control of their life and achieve the success they deserve.

1. Successful People and Leaving Nothing to Chance

YOU HAVE HEARD IT BEFORE BUT IT NEEDS TO BE SAID
'If you fail to plan you plan to fail!'

Success is not a guaranteed condition, and it requires continuous effort, planning, and adaptation to change. Successful people plan every aspect of their lives, leaving nothing to chance. They take calculated risks, embrace new ideas and concepts, and understand the importance of hard work, dedication, and perseverance. Moreover, they surround themselves with supportive individuals who can offer guidance and opportunities for growth. By following these principles, anyone can achieve success in their personal and professional lives. The belief that once you have achieved success, it will be roses and butterflies forever will be the first step to your downfall. Planning is a critical component of success. Successful people plan every aspect of their lives, from their daily routines to their long-term goals. They leave nothing to chance and understand that even the smallest details can make a significant difference in achieving their objectives. Knowing where your target is, and every avenue that is available and/or required to get there is what allows you to be able to take what are called calculated risks. Such risks are often essential to success. Successful people

understand that the risk of standing still is often greater than the risk of trying something new. They are willing to take risks and embrace new ideas and concepts. They also recognize the importance of letting go of old ideas and ways of doing things to make room for new, more effective approaches. Innovation and progress stem from having an insatiable appetite for advancement. But no amount of new products, trends, and concepts will be of use to you if you have no plan or no road map. Successful people are always at the forefront of change, constantly seeking out new ideas and ways to improve themselves and their businesses. The same principles of planning ahead also apply to money and finance. It is important to develop habits that will set you up to win. Being frugal, not stingy, is pivotal. habit. It means being mindful of your spending and avoiding wastefulness. This will make you more efficient with your money. Prioritize thriftiness, avoiding waste. Save more than they spend, which leads to financial success. Comparison-shop, negotiate, avoid overspending, and leave nothing to chance. This is not a license to be cheap, Get the right thing the first time. The right tool for the job is not always the most expensive but cheap will always fail you in the end.

Remember, cheap now is expensive later.
Success does not come overnight it comes over several nights!!
Planning and taking calculated risks are not the only pathway to prosperity. Hard work, dedication, and perseverance are the characteristics required to sustain over time.
No one is an island You must also understand that there is strong

networking and collaboration. Surround yourself with like-minded individuals who can offer support, advice, and growth opportunities. They also seek out mentors and coaches who can provide guidance and help them stay focused on their goals.

Scientific studies show that the brain is designed to set and pursue goals. This fact should plant the seed that nudges you towards goal setting so you can't simply desire success, you must make a definitive internal and outward declaration of what you want to achieve.

The subconscious mind will strive tirelessly to attain whatever you declare. So set challenging yet achievable goals that you can track, measure, and diligently work towards them daily.

2. Be Observant And Inspired

Being observant and inspired is a powerful phrase that emphasizes the importance of paying attention to the world around you and seeking inspiration from various sources. By being observant, you can identify new opportunities and emerging trends, which will help you make better decisions and Increase your likelihood of positive results. By seeking inspiration, you will be able to draw upon diverse perspectives and leverage the collective wisdom of others. this will provide more insights that can spark new ideas. In both your personal and professional lives, being observant and inspired can help you stay ahead of

the curve.

Aside from having it in for cats, curiosity is extremely useful! Curiosity is the foundation of creativity. The more curious you are, the more creative you become. To tap into your natural curiosity, ask more questions instead of making quick decisions. Often, we make decisions based on what has worked or not worked in the past, but in today's constantly changing world, this approach can be misleading. It's important to pause and ask more questions about the problem or solution. Ask questions like "why," "what if," or "why not?" to open up new possibilities and explore fresh solutions.

When you ask questions that begin with "why," "what if," or "why not?", it encourages you to think beyond your current perspective and consider new possibilities.

For example, asking "why" can help you understand the root cause of a problem or challenge, and guide you toward finding a more effective solution. "Why is this happening?" or "Why do I feel this way?" are good examples of starting with "why."

Asking "what if" can help you explore alternative scenarios and possibilities that you may not have considered before. For instance, "What if we approach this problem from a different angle?" or "What if we tried a completely new strategy?"

"Why not" questions encourage you to challenge assumptions and

consider taking risks that you may have been hesitant to take before. For example, "Why not try a new approach to this project?" or "Why not take a chance on this new opportunity? By asking these types of questions, you can break out of old habits, think more creatively, and discover new approaches that can lead to success.
Ultimately, being observant and inspired is a powerful mindset that can help us reach our full potential and make a positive impact on the world around us.

3. Prioritize Health Mental and Physical Unlocking Your Full Potential

Keep educating yourself via school. Personal

learning and being observant of what is around you. Look,

the world is ever-changing, and it's important to keep learning not only to stay up-to-date but to get ahead of the latest trends and technologies. Your mind which can be taken from you is the best tool for staying in front of the curve and self-improvement. This fundamental habit makes you more adaptable which is crucial in this fast-paced world we live in. Your ability to adjust quickly to new situations and circumstances is how you will thrive. With a strong mind, new ideas and approaches won't Intimidate you. Cognitive development unlocks your potential.

It is no secret that maintaining good physical and mental health is an integral part of being successful. A healthy body and mind can lead to greater achievements, increased energy, and productivity, boosted self-confidence and self-esteem, and a longer and more fulfilling life. Maintaining good physical health is a crucial part of being successful in life. It allows us to perform our daily tasks at a higher level because our blood is flowing and giving proper distribution. You find yourself better equipped to effectively handle your daily responsibilities, leading to greater achievements and avoiding reduced performance levels. Additionally, good mental health is essential for overall well-being. Allow time to let yourself know that you are a good person and that good things come to you... That is a form of manifestation and meditation called a positive daily mantra. The reason that it is effective is that the repetition of these types of things works on your subconscious Repeating positive affirmations can have a great impact on your brain because it fires up your neural pathways. The effects are a happy and positive mood. It can activate certain areas of your brain that make you feel happier and more positive. Studies have also shown that using affirmations decreases health-deteriorating stress and promote exercise, healthy eating habits, and success in academics. Various studies also confirm affirmations: which are always running in the background helping to guide the moves and decisions we make.

Conversely, if you told yourself regularly that "I can't," "I don't have talent," "I'm ugly," "I'm stupid" or "I'm useless." you will get results that match your sentiment. You will subconsciously self-sabotage. So keeping a positive mental mantra is one of the best things you can do for yourself.

Also, avoid at all costs self-deprecating humor for its effect are increased levels of stress and anxiety. When you make negative comments about yourself, it reinforces negative self-perceptions and leads to a cycle of negative self-talk. This can increase feelings of stress and anxiety, and may even contribute to the development of depression. Remember your subconscious will operate on what your conscious says.

Hey, we want SUCCESS not DEPRESS!

Another secret tip is that you should examine the people with whom you associate because people who have given up can't encourage you to do better because they don't know how they are broken and destitute. Don't forget misery loves company. Align yourself with those who are heading your direction or are already there you will increase your chances of winning 10 fold.

A healthy lifestyle can increase energy levels and productivity. The physical fitness enables individuals to handle challenges more efficiently, leading to greater success. So as you can see a healthy body and mind can boost self-confidence and self-esteem, essential factors for achieving success. People who feel good about themselves are more likely to pursue their goals and take risks. When you function at the highest levels, your bodies require proper maintenance, similar to a machine. Hence, successful people make it a point to eat healthily and exercise regularly. Starting the day with protein, fiber, and good fats for fuel is crucial, followed by an alkaline diet rich in green veggies, nuts, and whole grains for sustained energy and focus.

Good health and fitness can increase longevity and allow individuals to enjoy life to the fullest. On the other hand,
poor health can limit opportunities and lead to missed chances, resulting in
an unfulfilling *life.*

4. Focus Stay True to YOUR Own Path Avoiding Distraction

The life of your dreams requires a belief in your capabilities. Making conscious choices every day with the end goal in mind even if it is not in sight. In my extensive interviews with hundreds of extremely effective individuals, most of them revealed they weren't the most naturally gifted or skilled in their field. However, they made the deliberate decision to believe that anything is possible and put in the hard work and dedication without excuses. You see winners possess a mindset of self-confidence and approach their aspirations with the attitude that they can achieve them.

Be resolute in your pursuits.

The award goes to those who possess

the habit of focusing on what truly matters. There is a sea of various compelling distractions, competing and in some cases demanding you pay them attentionYou can only snatch the crown if you have unyielding, unwavering focus, and a refusal to compromise on your commitment. Setbacks and failures are natural but focus and resilience require a purpose. Once you find your purpose, your ability to bounce back and continue moving forward is as easy as SAID & DONE. Small tips to help you recognize some of the small distractions that can hinder you from focusing on your goal making it harder to reach them:

Bonus Tips for Focus

Every time you check your phone for a pointless text or turn on the TV to watch your favorite show, you are losing precious time that could be spent pursuing your goals. To avoid these distractions, turn off notifications and keep your phone out of reach. By doing this, you will be able to focus on your work and complete tasks more efficiently.

Do you find yourself constantly checking your phone for messages or scrolling through social media? These distractions can significantly reduce your productivity and prevent you from achieving your goals. To overcome this, turn off sound notifications and keep your phone in another room. By minimizing distractions, you will be able to complete tasks quicker and have more time for leisure activities.

Prioritize Your Time

Do you struggle to complete tasks within your desired timeframe? Distractions like text messages and television can significantly reduce your productivity and impact your ability to achieve your goals. To minimize these distractions, turn off notifications and avoid turning on the TV when you have work to do. By prioritizing your time and minimizing distractions, you can accomplish more in a shorter amount of time.

5. Live Each Day Like Its TheLast. Embrace Each Day with Enthusiasm

That does not mean going off half-cocked!

If you want to live life to the fullest and make the most of every moment, it's important to go above and beyond. This means doing more than what's expected of you and giving your all in everything you do. Whether it's at work, school, or in your personal life, putting in the extra effort can lead to rewards like loyalty, referrals, and new opportunities.

Instead of focusing on what you can get out of a situation, try to focus on how you can exceed expectations and provide value. Do your best or better and give it your all. By doing so, you'll not only feel a sense of pride and fulfillment, but you'll also be setting yourself up for triumph. The energy you put out is what you get back, you know the equal and opposite reaction concept of motion. You want to live life to the fullest, understand that simply knowing isn't going to cut it,- you need to put it into action. Believe in yourself, and move with purpose towards your desired outcome.

1. Start making progress toward what you want to achieve.

2. Engage in activities that bring you closer to your desired result.

When you start taking action, you'll encounter situations that can broaden your understanding, perspective, and valuable lessons that you may not have learned otherwise. These experiences you can't find in books or from other people. You'll find like-minded people who are attracted to your aura, and who will support and encourage you. Hey, nothing happens until you take action. Those who make the most of their time recognize the power of showing appreciation to the people who support them, whether they be colleagues, loved ones, or employees. By acknowledging the contributions of others, they cultivate a supportive network that helps them achieve their goals.

In closing

- Be a purpose-driven individual who understands the importance of knowledge for achieving success.
- Prioritize personal growth and development.
- Harness your exceptional creativity and originality.
- Take ownership and responsibility for your actions.

- Always live in the present moment and seize opportunities as they arise.

- Be a tenacious spirit and never give up on your goals.

By examining these characteristics of high achievers, we can gain insights into what it takes to achieve success. Adopting these habits and practices can help us reach our own goals and aspirations.

Insights from various fields such as business, sports, and personal development divulge that high achievers tend to have certain habits and practices that contribute to their success. The key factor is their mindset, which differentiates high achievers from others. Generally, high achievers possess a growth mindset, which means that they believe in their abilities and develop them by putting in hard work and perseverance. Moreover, they view challenges as opportunities to grow rather than as obstacles that deter them from their desired destiny. Their resilience is remarkable as they can quickly recover from setbacks and failures.

However, behaviors are also equally important. It is not just about positive thinking and affirmations. One should be goal-oriented and proactive, taking conscious action towards achieving their objectives. It is vital to prioritize time and energy effectively, focus on what is most important and delegate non-essential tasks. High achievers are self-disciplined, consistently putting in the work required to achieve their goals.

Lastly, routines play a significant role in the success of high achievers. They usually follow structured schedules, which enable them to concentrate on their most important tasks at the most productive times of the day. They also prioritize self-care such as exercise and meditation, which helps to maintain their energy and mental focus.

Examining these mindset, behavior, and routine factors can provide valuable insights into what makes successful people. Adopting these habits and practices can increase our own chances of success and enable us to achieve our goals.